p0sthuman

the evening before

Front cover image by Jorge Simmons-Valenzuela courtesy Unsplash.
Cover concept and back cover image by Peter Jerrim.
Photo of Peter Jerrim by Alastair Bett.

Design, typesetting and printing management by Burringbah Books, 23 Hobart Road, South Launceston, Tasmania 7249.

ISBN: 978 0 645089 37 0

Peter Jerrim was born in Tasmania in 1948. He taught primary and secondary students for 24 years. In 1990 he published his first science fiction book for teenagers. In 1994 he went on to write full time, creating axel-and-alice, a 7000-page hypertext novel. As a first-of-its-kind, a web version was archived by the National Library of Australia. From 2000 Peter developed websites and wrote content for business, healthcare and educational enterprises. For his first volume of poetry he has selected poems he wrote between 1991 and 2022.

Acknowledgements

BLUE DOG Australian Poetry Vol 4 No 8 November 2005 for the first publication of 'adept at it' and 'well look who's here'

Frances Crick for the phrase 'every accident is frozen' in 'on the origin of' which is expanded from the original 'frozen accident' in Frances Crick 'The Origin of the Genetic Code' *Journal of Molecular Biology* Volume 38, Issue 3, 28 December 1968, Pages 367–379

Alan Ginsburg for the title of 'boxcars boxcars' derived from the longer phrase 'boxcars boxcars boxcars' in Allen Ginsberg *Howl, and other poems introduction by William Carlos Williams*, City Lights Books, 1959

Olivier Messiaen for titles from 'Vingt Regards sur l'Enfant-Jesus' (after personal discussion with the composer in 1988) as used in the nine selected 'Regards' poems on pages 142–150 in this volume

John Milton for the setting from the first scene of his masque *Comus* (1634) which precedes the content of the poem 'message in a bottle'

Elias Owen for the title of the poem 'on the origin of old stone crosses of the Vale of Clwyd' derived from his *Old Stone Crosses of the Vale of Clwyd and Neighbouring Parishes* London, Bernard Quaritch 1886; also the last stanza of the poem is quoted entire from page 216

Don Paterson for the phrase 'warm box' used as 'warm dry box' in 'Antares 2', being part of his analogy of the 'flimsy conceit' of a home in Don Paterson *The Poem: Lyric, sign, metre* Faber & Faber, 2018

to Penny

for waiting so long

Contents

pOsthuman
the evening before

Peter Jerrim

p0sthuman

there's an O in Object I fall thrOugh
and in Old and gOds
One day they'll be kept warm
in fOlds
and sOmetime Over a rainbOw
yOu'll appear with me On
the Other side Of the O
and lOOking back we'll
nOtice we fOrgOt
what it was like
o o o
where we came frOm

improbable romance 1

tickled by the Kentucky sward
at night we made love
on every golf course
in the county

as Venus throbbed in the east
we drank from each other's mouths
and pumped like dogs

cried like birds

afterwards we tuned our devices
to visitor radio
and wandered hand in hand
beneath the trees the stars

the breeze dried us

one moonlit night a joke
about cosmetic surgery turned
serious I got a razor from my kit
we cut one another

laid out on the
eighth hole
we inscribed pure math
in our flesh

coins
became crop circles
left scars like rope

infinite forms
of the prairie
tuned inward

fragmenter

then all the thoughts I'd dropped
in the too hard basket

opened before me like
the eyes of the cat I drowned in the river

along with her kittens their ballet
in the cage they were trapped in

animated my torchlight
like neon in Vegas

so I called it startup cantata
or the sucklings denied

(coins buried in jars
pay for their own funeral)

that sad plover cry at 2am
outbids a bronzewing for moonlight

their songs in the wind
wait like wet paint to unfurl

don't stare up at them rudely
just blink and receive

improbable romance 6

on Monday morning through the cracks
in the barn wall slopes of light
(they're sheets of paper stacked on edge)
illuminate an antique cultivator

and lovers who squirm
on a canvas-backed rug
thrown over hay bales

the motes of the dust of which are
whales rising slow in their heaven
sounding great notes
and silences

within the channels
and pulsing vesicles of the humans
neurones sparkle play

provisional jazz
from which
subsonic grunts and fumbles
are historic events

for the bacteria and phages
stuck in the mucus
that lubricates their tangle

and the crystals of iron
in the tines of the cultivator
are snap frozen fluorescences
stelae inscribed with flowers

on a dark
temple
in Memphis

switched off in 1958
a Silent Knight refrigerator
with no door
tilts one degree

it's stacked with paint tins
a radio on the top
bleats Slim Dusty (recently deceased)

and Little Pattie
(rereleased)
we could zoom in forever on
the details of this scene

and forget about the lovers
her and him and
who we think they are

just fifteen and
doing it quick
before the school bus
comes

after we met

we lay on the
bed

it snowed
that's all

then in the shower
the radio droplets were

source code
for your nearness

with which you propagated
errors into the universe

that you could not recall
while your voluptuous

thoughts
bent light rays

to bend
my mind

to bend the future
into what I guess

was your will, and so
it snowed

and the hush
of your after

thoughts
remains

difference between chocolate

go on
tell me what you're going to tell me
then tell me
then tell me what you told me
the middle bit being chocolate the outer bits
your forefinger
and thumb conveying it to your mouth
from which come ruined notes
and desolation
while miraculously my claymation heart keeps beating

rookie reward

your eyes colosseums
never to be renovated
my heart
a ukulele club
on stage too soon

ok,

hit me with the blunt
instrument of your
nakedness

your heel on my head
your distant
laugh

because when you wear clothes
you confuse me
with endless words

your candied tongue's
a breach of light
ground

into glitter
it makes my necessary past
unnecessary now

espousal

night and
nude opens fridge

onto railway lines
onto mozart's

train crash
concerti

sudden enough
(and other stuff in infinite loops)

to push fright
under your heart again

histories
shouting themselves into history

though your voice
round with pebbles

groans
for oxygen repurposed

while inconsolable beings
husband few clouds

Aristotle contemplating a bust of Homer

these knuckles
bare worlds
graze your face

leave bruised songs
yellowing towards light
and culpability

the glass paperweight
you threw at my head
had read my thoughts

through its trajectory

as each tear

as

each tear exploded
stars
on your face
your makeup

revealed a
parallel paradise
in which you played
only yourself

but then the change
before dawn
the stutter of rain
in a steel land

tiny we were
before the torment the tempest
wailing
desperate for each other

in progress

the bullet's a book furrowing
moonlight into occupied france
grazing the slough of lives long gone

down lanes of arcady
bared by the ploughboy's gaze

look back from your carriage
the moonlight's streaming
through poplars satyrs in marble

a temple glimpsed by poussin
remember that cold voluptuary

you brushed leaves from her lips
then kissed them
there was no fire but

what burnt within you
it still burns will burn forever

strafing the under storeys
blazing with homeward desire
the bullet's a book you're reading it

in hospital corridors at night too late
to examine for tracers of life

1950

intimate as aspirational your voice
misinterprets coffee, smoke
though a skylight the timeline
it Tarzans by unzips into eloquence

because if you were naked for export
you'd be believed
as easily as I
by my dearly beloved the sky's

deep rockets sundering
but I was blind
to their motive
shading your thought bubbles grey

Huey Dewey Louie
argue for fame
after frame
they have no plan for the suction

unnarrating movies of green
rolling hills
no storyline
dialogue characters simply viridian

shades and sharps while
your antennae scan
for anomalies
from this kitchen window forever

taverner, then tye

that I can't hear a damn thing
without
the renaissance surface

of these bubbles and the torpedoes
below
zinging with heat

is pleasantly disconcerting, to say
the least – the trebles like
tuning forks bearing so many degrees to glissando

from the mean – I suppose it's an effect
like moving from one room
to another

or from autumn to winter,
sky to
wet horizon

or like this company
singing, blended glad and
sangfroid all at once

if you wander into them
without instructions
you run the risk

of needles in your ears
perhaps
your eyes

room's soft doors

vague bills
light bells
and you tell me
wait for the radiance

though the heat's
in my head too late
too far from my heart
too sotto voce

so the quilts
the means of time
fold me warm and
mathematical

for what's
this all about
but that everything
so simple counts

Billie

you're an inflammatory comment
slouched at the lights
waiting to cross the road

face stripped bare
to every car
your legs (god, legs!) arrest me

high school slut
you in a short dress
no socks

do nothing to please me
except what keeps you
occupied

I'll watch
in the rear mirror, look at you
later

so you'll endure?
cleave?
cut your losses?

your mother's obduracy
your father's
mind

they're absorbed
in the olive
within you

your father's other lives
your mother's
lies

I've seen her
push the flesh
into place

when I come
to your
door

like you
she won't take no
for an answer

lighter than heir

parachuted
into the present
straight away I

check out the
talent
(yeah, they'd said,

don't imagine you'll
be in a super mall
when you resolve

naked in front
of surprised
shoppers)

so the dark horse says,
well, hello horse,
(aargh, I think, I

thought I would
at least
be human

but there's this
black horse sidling
up to me, nuzzling…)

hello gorgeous
hello stranger
it's strangely

disconcerting
but it's the work
of a moment to be

the hot horse
I truly am
in my present

tense (it's no good
thinking, once
I was a god

in the preexisting
age
of gods,

it's better to be
a horse being
penetrated by another horse

right now
albeit
but briefly

than a genius
empty of flesh
and filled

with infinite time
on the in
side

and no
outside
to speak of)

annunciation after Richter after Titian

the night of the
and the return
the semblance

my womb
   violetly
irradiated with

but. particularly your feet did
not touch
and the genesis

only a graphed moment
before time
   again

rapidly willingly
swellingly
after the

   invaded

near life (experience)

you're deep in shit
code warrior
in a house in a house in a house
drenched with blood
then dried and
powdered with galaxies
when will you stir
blind man?
when will you
chew cigarette hills
choke on bison up to their dewlaps in honey?
or smell daylight
bookcases of it
ready for fingering
can you hear the automobiles
pass in the rain?
once you were carried in one
something warm like a woman
sat next to you
spoke mother words
deep in the dark
they curve
you remember…
angels and crows crowd hills
and midges circle
it's late afternoon
you touch lichen
eat snow
but you thirst
for more than the sun
you're deep in grace
code warrior
blind man
empty balloon
automaton

next cab off the rank

late October 2005, Pennington County
walking uphill through white weather
unseasonably warm
I come across a woman who
works out
eschews alcohol
has three lovers
none of whom
knows of the others
hopes to get pregnant
by one of 'em
is forty something
it's probably
too late
she's been there done
that
held down jobs on both sides of the world
one of which
wouldn't seem likely for such a diminutive
lady
physics professor
crocodile wrangler, country and western
warbler, librarian
for a theosophist in Kensington
a body building legend's
masseuse
she tells me all this in the space
of a few minutes, you know
how it is, when you meet someone in passing
share microorganisms
admire the view without comment, find
you're swapping philosophies
histories, I

surreptitiously
take her photo
when her back
is turned
it's late October 2005, Pennington County
walking downhill through white weather
unreasonably
warm

always October (2005)

in the wave front that's a spiral arm of this
corporate
citizen's watch
in the ellipse of the ellipse of its galactic
orbit
far out far out far out
on this solar
citizen's
watch
which next time
it comes around won't
be
travelling west in Pennington County 2005 where
gods cheer the twilight
and gesture
(benevolent)
as I arm wrestle
spirals
winding me winding me up
and all in a fall towards night they cry
long lonesome cowboy calls
and coyotes how how howling
they slide towards October
2005
time and again and again
don't you think they've had enough of it
got enough of it
those wah-wah warriors frequenting the skies
out on a limb in October
with all those cries all that cries wolves
and their crimes and their lackadaisacal
attitudes
towards men and meat and me and the opportune
skies

now U R 6

on the fridge
in marker pen mark

an equation
or a few

instantly that turbulent
stream is a pool

where quolls sip
starlight

or an archaeopteryx
pecks roadkill

OK, wunderkind
for your next trick

reach back through your singularity
to the preexisting conditions

pull from your hat
that sleek and struggling rabbit

contingency
don't heed the audience's gasps

the squeaks and pops
of flattop reality

being unpacked
screwed upright

varnished
lent upon

proceed
into the infinity of your mind

just a kid
still got your baby teeth

what would your mother say
if she could see you now

quite a magician
you little lizard

with wings

silence of the crows

on-screen I climb
habitué of sunlight
into a sorta zen

rubato the wine
pours
by my neighbour

who's not embarrassed by
our pie in the sky
hi fivin' lifestyle

slapping our eyes onto
mags and movies
the blue view ahead

and our ears into
in-flight telephony
we're occupied

while terrorists tick
and hues continue
to zing

round this round
poor excuse for an
earth

I'd be satisfied
with Saturday in a caf
in the high street

or malling around in the dark
waiting for that goddam
electra

to burst forth in wrong
any chance of a chat
show hostess turning up

in the third act
played by dame someone
who oughta be younger

not pied or a paid up
political wench
someone straighter

and slick
a musical
nouveau guru

interrupting my
after dinner
apnea

with blogs from the periphery
and antediluvian
clatter

time was
when this sorta thing
was in character

curiously
those crows who made so much clamour
at nightfall are quiet now

'boxcars boxcars'

analog scream

the last smooth thing
and everything changes

the pool of blood
the blonde

though it's pleasant enough strolling through woods not far
    from a home in the moonlight, the scent of tobacco
    in the air (I was there) it was 1954

or before

I could tell when I read them, the poets, the ones I
    understood, the ones who understood themselves, those
    who understood neither (I was one) it was

analog summer

when bees in bells hammered interiors
and warm days rang

we were importunate then
cultured from a line of stem cells traced back to the
    Doomsday Book

the rape in the fields
the yellow of Europe
revealed

analog hours

when fortunes are read
as we rush by torchlight into the night and the

clanging

adept at it

you're a line drawing bureaucrat
in the periodical Punch the squirl of
your nose incomplete a teenager
stares at you in a dentist's
waiting room
in 1964 you didn't ask
to be drawn

or a butterfly tat
on a girl's shoulder in 2000 you're
here for the long haul petty monkey
gluing through bars with her slipping
haikus into drinks
that can't be
true

you're a bear walking out of the
woods in a New Yorker cartoon
in 19
57 now
incinerated deciphered
don't search back issues or archives
you're just a breath

or a poem you're
sound waves
seeking an ear in Midlothian
or Melbourne you're the
perfect white of your mother's
thighs
rustling

not drowning

are you ever going to be
where I want you to be

in a shard of green light
in cézanne

in a chopper
a mottled cliff at 3 o'clock

below
grey sea

useless the colour of guts
and all that's inside me

in the dark for decades
then squandered in sunshine

cinematic dystopias
the slow wine

of ancient hypertexts
ambiguous lines

drift through an under
ground carpark

it's in your dream, your movie
black limos glide

a star
on each side

impasto of tyre hush
and the thud of car doors

we pass
steel elevator doors

a slow ghost
bends, a shopping bag

her child
in a pusher

strings, unisons
a slow beat, sixths

somewhere
mortal flesh

falls
silent

improbable romance 5

back in '94
Lissi lies in her huggie harem soft toy paradise
her piping voice
filters to the adults who dine
at nine

Lissi discovered the Web today, says Amanda, listen...

+ click Barbie

  + click Posh

    + click teddy

      + click ALL my favourites

        + click pillow

        + click dream

click dick
thinks Tove, says

Welcome to the hypertextual universe ladies and gents
    where every thread's a winner and...
pedestrians on fire have only to think the word HELP before
    none arrives

Jason pours more wine, steers his smile towards the kitchen
Mel yawns and the dog under the table suddenly understands
what they're all on about

those voices banging in her ears the shuffling thighs
    the must the musk…interpreting toes
she yelps, her pentecost's complete, within weeks
    she'll read letters
then correspond with stars

meanwhile Tove does his
fantastic plastic
trick
swallows his Mastercard
nods as he counts to five

Always wanted to be a plastic surgeon, says Amanda as
    Tove vomits the gleaming card onto the table
Or a brain surgeon, says Mel

it doesn't seem possible but the card is bent

Jason returns with paper towel to blot the spit and sick,
    thinks…

creatures of untrammelled beauty populate my dreams
yet I'm awake
and driving
across a bridge that seems to end in sky
kiss me anywhere
and I'll expire
in a white hot field
among white words
where only one is pink

Lucky I got plenty of 'em, says Tove and whips a deck
of credit cards from his pocket
anyone for bridge?
a flutter on the geegees?
top up your super?
or your tank?

Time for dessert? says Amanda

Mel looks at Tove her wrist

I'll tuck Lissi in, says Jason

in her room
toys stare
into the penumbra
around the night light glow

+ click Daddy, says Lissi

  + click me

Nigh nigh Lissi
says Daddy

let creatures of untrammelled beauty
populate your dreams

improbable romance 17

you rammed your fingers down my throat
and dragged out a map of England
which, spread before us glistening,
revealed elfin fires, a ruined abbey
and Heathrow

the parasite of my future thus extirpated
you turned your attention below
one hand worked my bandolier
the other poured
heavy guitars

pissed psalmist, daubing the skies
with red before sunrise
you're stuck in a circle of days
you should be on fire
burning DNA, calm and sequestered

then
at the next election
when your white smoke rises
the weight of the world
will slip from your shoulders again

considering

my panopticon
state of mind
my

specialist work (when I can get it) as a wannabe royal
being the work of the ego the work of a moment
to inhale only bubbles exhaled

by other wannabes
their CO_2 levels
their viral loads rising under

my babbling breath
held a few minutes then
my head bursts

through a lake of blood.
in my first trimester
a heart beat

and on you went
uninterrupted and
hundreds of megalitres later I say thanks

for your good work
your reliability, if only
you could continue

a bit longer
powering this fool in paradise this
novelty toy

this me

message in a bottle

The first sceane discovers a wild wood, then a guardian spiritt
or demon descendes or enters.

– John Milton, Comus, 1634

do I mean it?
the obscurity

the fog of vehicle licence plates
barcodes radio frequency identification tags hermeneutic

coruscations along chattering borders
hamletic inversions

fires@night.com
now I don't need running or religion any more

and even music's lost its sting and solace
medical science?

I gotta hold on a bit longer
but snow and the silver slate sea

the mountain at dawn
parrots

clouds
the perfume of a woman in a lane in London

about the time of
my life

my wife eats breakfast cereal in bed at 2am

on that infinite shore
next door
chim

chim
the spoon bowl
pages turn

hyperacusis of sheets
stirred bed
clothes

and the starry
shutters
shut

through which I feel my life
i.e. my
self & other fatuous

ampersands
endure
musket fire from heaven

milk wars

which are all in your head, I think
trailing ectoplasm, sluicing the burbs
while cutlery clanking in drawers cries
hold me

so the porter, the door, the nervous
fruit loop dreaming never quite reaching
the parade ground
(though there are benefits

in mortality you found it not such
a clever trick) the scene select loop (and
sure there are other loops,
like the blind snaps up, the beautiful

lumen
the milk of lumin
osity)
saying rap

idly her
ovaries one two one two one
craning the sky
the daynight never stops

back from Bali

back from Bali we make our own
shadow show… out of the

flickering my silhouette
cowboy in slo mo rides

his dangling head a comet
that trails slight light…

your bar girl cleans the saloon,
slops from a pail then steps in it…

her feet splash my matinee
idol, his

number's up he trembles,
draws erect and pulls on a cigar…

off the smoky coast
beacons slide into dark

you've had enough
and reach for the remote

I catch your sticks…
keep jiggling

towards Amy

'Permanent disequilibria threaten'
(not clouds on the horizon
or lightning seen through
your forehead
or the tide rising higher
than you think it used to

but significant perturbations
of your spine's
timeline and a strange taste
in your mouth). Now you
turn to me with that
shattered look you're a past

master of, your dress creased
from too much sitting,
your fingers crossed in
anxiety. It's the age
of middens again,
mountains of shells

from which the flesh has
been filched, and what's
left of your blue eyes
berate me.
But what can I do?
I ate my fill long ago.

The pain passes. I see
you again as you
want to be seen, the heat
from your body
cogent,
and instantly I remember

how you tore your clothes
for fear of
the geography of lead
ships under stars
and rehearsals
of icebergs.

These days I hear you
singing in half
familiar tongues
before I see you
rising through bodies
not yours, the weight

of the trains
you have travelled in
not holding you down.
I gape at your effrontery,
back from the dead with no
qualms. Perhaps

you have a chance to
live again. It has only
been me
holding you back. Come,
put your hand here
in the fire and be free.

touchdown

on every square millimetre
of your surface
your toes depended

a wild family
of moons
soles scrawled

with messages about limits
of divorce
and divinity

and up your legs which are more memories
than travelling companions
being

responsible, their beauty catalogued,
their genius to
walk, but now,

a pink brown lack
of discernment, then blandness, and forward to
glistening disorder

all these hectares and I have not yet found
a blemish
wild I cried,

kissing your absences
and profoundly
asleep

to everything
on the other side
of your skin

triumph of venus

chop that trumpet call
& reassemble it

as a lunar tune
an anthem in reverse

from imagined corners
choirs home in

all hollows mourn
and dolphins draw

a supermodel
on a scallop shell

who yodels
as the wind thuds in her ears

her page boy
blows a conch

you hear
the battle fluids

of a republic
sequestered, dark

and sparkling
or whatever fluids do

mind ½ full

½ asleep I am
when a ½ naked

fat lady
on a stool

whisks off her
panties in

½ a second
& the fat man

next   to   me

is astonished
like me

@her Speed
her

dex
terity

her copious
skin

&
the fact that

there is no blemish
as far in

as 1's eye can
see

up at sparrow fart (circa 2000)

at breakfast at the High Chaparral
totally chilled passionate dudes
munch bloomsday burgers
pour powder snow on cereal metonymy

their cigar and dope smoke levitates
an elfin pinnace to hum among the rafters
ufologists' muse, the tiny captain coughs
drops an anchor into an eye below

gotcha! the dudes wheeze and blink
empathising with the kitchen hand
who struggles with the hook
that's pierced his retina

his very soul's on fire
it's drawn out, attenuated, snapped and scanned
then released
and while he grovels on the floor

the captain rubs his databanks
and pulls his pinnace to the shore
(the chasing along the flange
around the hood above the stove)

dudes cringe and cuss
then shave and shit
and, steady for the day
stretch limbs outside

call hello hello
to echoing hills
embraced by azure rings
of smoke from ranges far

cabaret

bees in poppies
ants in a cabinet
of blond wood laminated lacquered sixties short splayed
    legs brass feet on the
left pulled outward and down from the top edge a door opens
a record player slides out-and-down on hinged grooves that
    keep it horizontal
the rolling stones on the turntable spin
the tonearm bobs up and down the stylus runs in a 500 metre
    single etched spiral groove to sing
I CAN'T GET NO O SAT
IS FACTION
on the right a door's pulled out-and-down from the top edge
revealing a radio with an amber dial on which a cream
    coloured plastic indicator runs through
9LO but you don't know what's there because the record
    player is selected
I CAN'T GET NO O
GIRLY ACTION
neither can you hear through a sash window of 3 mm float glass
on the edge of the suburb a distant beach's bleak waves
    through which dolphins
dance
nor indeed your neighbours talking

no good reason

faux torso twister
lightning phases

with those glia gleaming
there's an idea in there somewhere

of words that are on and are my mind
by wattle birds in a red gum in

September

start up start up start up quick
start up start up start up quick

start up start up start up quick
start up start up start up quick

forthwith forthwith forthwith
forthwith forthwith forthwith

fuck fuck fuck fuck
pour quoi pour quoi

chant de tasmanie

into
a song field
with many solutions
your mouth
opens

your sisters
slap water
on the off beat
apprising
the light

their bare feet
beat
over oyster beds
or push through cutting grass
into uplands

where cloudlines dream
on the haze of
mauve mountains
oceans desire
to lap over them

hoons in the valleys
rejoice
their flatulent V8s
boast
of angst and a past

the felt
tips of evening
finger the family the
notes
in their heads

I have not heard
or truly seen
the silver wattles
their generous
drifts

or wallabies in the night wind
dim among stars
only ours
for the naming

this day this door

this day this door
throw me through it

into the storm bloopers
how'd they infiltrate my

reality show
and poison every minute? the

ratings plummeted and
while extremely watching

fractals you
ruined my redemption

improbable romance 8

you trickled heroin into condoms and swallowed them
I packed 40 years of television into a single night
we both exploded
they flushed us off the tiles with a fire hose
all that was left were the memories
streaming down the gutters of time
beaming out to the constellations
it's quiet out there
your bits and mine
mingled diluted divine
evaporating with the square of the distance
travelled
since 1999

arrested development

like, this possum in its anxiety runs 50 metres along the top
   of this paling fence, at least I think it's anxious, it
   obviously doesn't want to touch the ground, being
   startled by me, my footsteps on gravel coming out of the
   darkness, then its mate, its sibling whatever, scrabbles
   also, the same 50 metres, from darkness to darkness...

my fingers, thus, tremble on you

one hand plays your extremity, that is, your skin, your
   membrane billowing under the steady pressure of, for
   want of a better word,

time

the other hand plays the piano, your mind, dreaming a
   crowded harbour of triathletes, all stamped with an
   indelible mark, thrashing

hamming it up

all day on the kitchen bench where I left it the glass of water
with a slice of lemon in it hurtles through a medium with
which I am not yet familiar

and all night

this morning when we woke I said I'll get in the shower and
nearly said the bath

which took me back to when we lived at Edith Creek on tank
water and we only had a bath with a few centimetres of
water to slip around in

nice to start the day dancing on your back

some winter mornings I had to push the car to start it on the
flat road past the dairy feet sliding on frost the last cows
still complaining this memory so real I nearly slid back
there to repeat those years and not keep hurtling through
this medium with which I am not yet familiar

when I was 13 the chassis of the radio I was building bent like
the wing of an angel under duress the valves were time
machines, resistors the soldiers I soldered into camaraderie
while the Voice of America boomed and the Voice of the
Andes and various Victor Romeos their confident ham
arcana crackling comfort while I turned the tuning dial

I was familiar with their sheds and basements with racks of
gear and the underscoring 50 hertz hum they talked
about their kids and caravans tracked sputniks listened
in to police and Yanks on military frequencies in a
medium with which I'm still not familiar though I did
discover Bach on three LPs and, though I thought I
understood it for a while, the St Matthew Passion

did not unlock it like I'd hoped

qui tollis peccata mundi

I stood in the swamp an agate in each hand and before me
    rose the laws of the universe in entangled skeins
pockets of light emptied in puddles, the slant of the sky
    spoke winter

the brew in the heads of the children around me arced, I
    could see they were angels
I choked on decipherable air
a verbose epiphany just a moment in bumble, small storms
    in small minds was enough

get back on the bus, I said
and they did, each with their agates, some would keep
    them for years or tumbled in tins become smooth as the
    gears of the world
others lost before bedtime or stolen by brothers became
    hidden whorls of desire

so much for field trips, or the mind of a man who stands at
    a window and stares

remembering children he taught three decades ago under stars

Friday lunchtime, Lindisfarne, 1979

red hot pokers take the name of their god in vain along a
  bank pushed up by a bulldozer ten years before they
blaze
behind them shrubbery masticates the breeze which soughs
  from the sea
innuendos of children ravel, play under pines, one of them
  screams
as an ant injects formic acid into his knee but no one notices
until a slow girl wanders over, normally a show pony who
  couldn't give a toss
the teachers are nowhere to be seen
the sun winks in the watery sky
someone puts down their coffee
the bitten child is bathed in several words, the effect being a
  layer of meaning clamped to his face
there's darkness coming
when the colour of blood is forgotten and the shape of a
  face blurs in the wind
it's the age of antibodies when nothing is sacred
and these kids will grow old with nothing to say
like the last patches of snow in Antarctica they'll be
untrammelled
by crocuses

neighbours in vertigo

to breathe is egregious in the age
of carbon
expelled from Eden
we wade through a limited palette
our feet drag
primary colours
mix them up marvellously

I could bury my head in your brain
and imagine streaks fluorescing
your spine
those little feet pretending
to be impulses
like a key on a kite before lightning
resisting your stare

teen gothic

that imagined space you'd
take up here if you were here
when it's chill night and your blond ghost's
infrared and real and I could grab you now

before at last
you're finally gone
and the wind
stops and your accident hasn't happened yet

tonight
when you fling your face
into the cold water of chance and breathe
it tears my lungs, too, and your facades are

printing everywhere
printing on me
that intimacy we knew
before we met and infinitely diverged

ironing

opened the ironing board
   poppy seed smells then
   sandalwood-ylang-ylang-jasmine
   My Sin
   dabbed on my wrists

   in '71

pressed the dress
   cupboard musk flowers expand me dream squares the
   Rothko Chapel

held it against me in front of the mirror the
   wireless Dionne Beatles Warwick Stones the Dylan Band
   Easybeats
   and Brahms
   sausage shafts sunshine mellow forest canopy Bavarian barns

Mahler's Titan looms my bedroom sunrise in jeans and
   nothing else in my white night dress my legs hot warned
   me about this
   and closed the ironing board

ounces of boyfriend wet nasturtiums tumbling from the shelf
   beach shells and I'm

trawling the void
   fragments of fish jetty no more Movietone the spindled
   segments of angels nuns softcover romance I'm

dragging the quantum vacuum
   abdominal wounds insist flavour of milkshakes Pepsi it's
   all about India
   why my father abandoned

granularity – and I'm breathing in leaves and at
   oh two hundred hours grey pilots leap from their bunks
   in one minute droning the channel they wish a
   photograph of diana/molly
   pressed
   in their pocket
   would protect ack ack the simulacrum the code in the
   night the radio silence
   and if they go down

there's a strong possibility cognitive affective impairment
   only the miraculous sonnets
   of Master Wu
   wine in an eggshell ink in a thimble
   …
   hard things to remember

when wakened at night your hand fumbles the phone heart
   pumps you know the news is

bad

and Eve

I'm the man who never was a boy
never had a toy
nor a mother

I've been putting files in wedding cakes
ever since I was
a boy
or a toy
or another

and I think

who'd pay more
than me

to take away
a life of joy

like this

in whose shoes now

my soles still ringing from walking barefoot on sharp stones
I put an ad on a dead social media account:
WANTED

FRIENDLY LIGHT PARTICLE
FOR VOYAGE
WITH MASSLESS HUMAN TRAVELLING AT

SPEED OF LIGHT
MUST BE ABLE TO SPEND A LONG TIME
IN VACUUM

although glass
is my preferred
medium

my face
in a
font

of
emerging
cognition

my font
in your
face

is the
thought
of

space
unseating
me

we're
n
tangled

your face a character
in all possible fonts
when a shotgun blast

spreads my brain
behind a stack of
magazines

the only thing about a
black hole
is its area

the only thing
about me is
flow

you choose
where
next

inventrix

they also
are a contender
for bi play
honours
I'm talking about
aeronautics here

no I'm not I'm
talking about collective
angst and wank on
election eve
wine glasses thrown into the fire
from which smoke

of several colours rises
that crystal had never held
the squeeze
the fruit of love
the fruit of
contention

duly done
the thing is
everything's an election
a summer of everything gone wrong
the shimmering discord
of all possible lies

then you wake
I hold your head
sweet chalice
warming memories
in only one
solution

proof (that flight is possible)

fake math | but what a pleasure to write it | why not | if it's a
    consistent world? | like fake fur | ok to touch | no blood

a long amalfi coast at dawn there are | equations | uberopolis
    |of integers | indefatigable | googolflops | more than
    enough for this | universe

yeah i saw grauballe man in springtime too | desiccated
    tanned | and silvered in my flash | his shocked red hair that
    black head twisted back | garrotted | in woodland
    monoculture | i ran and felt the sprites uncanned

it coulda been bobby kennedy there | or john f | from the
    grassy knoll | dreams rise

jackie she | half rises from her seat and turns | through this
    moment we should not watch | she's

lady luck | her neckline plunges | and in her box | a swamp of
    violins

then in london opposite the lyceum

a man a long beard throws bible high | it falls | it tries to fly |
    and crashes to the pavement | he shows the page it opens
    on | to girl black skirt | tucks it under arm | hurries | away

this guy i've never met before | and i | continue | wry

perhaps not particularly helpful advice to self

your cello
limply propelling
feng shui
nonsense into the naughty
cupboard where
number robbers run

and thereby hangs
your disgrace
your diminishing discriminancies
your variegated virtue
your canonical exigencies
your mosh pit between the ears excuses for inaction

and what to do when doing is to be done and done and done
to within a pit stop of your life
the electric vehicles in your gaming
firmament autonomous for now
just charge em up as quick as poss
and much ado about nothing much for
now just get it
done

bob, bill

you said the music would play all day but I didn't expect
   this, the microphones picking up every susurration, I
   don't think you had the slightest idea how that would
   affect me, well this is the result, every sound is a colour
   and every colour breaks into pieces, OK there are
   residues, finessed emotions, tips of angry continents like
   tips of leaves, if only I could resolve the meaning in your
   mind, because this is my mind and you are welcome to it

I said brothers who take matters into their own heads, that's
   us, that secret solidarity, compact to squeeze our heart

think nothing of it, you said, there's more where that came
   from, no weakness asked for and none expected

then grace is all I ask, I said

or footfalls on planets where no one comes

which anatomy lesson

which anatomy
lesson the one
in the copse, the leaves
drifting into the abdominal

cavity, or the one on the slab
dull but its still sinews
still sing our tune
or the one in the movie

which anatomy lesson
the one where your hand
lingers on cold organs
or the one where you lift

a heart
into clinical light

Kafka reads Kafka

it's not my fault said the key in the lock
in the dark
anyone could make the same mistake

an
atom
y's

a picnic with everyone's lips taped
their covert isolationist tactics
dim dirigibles

tho' I wore down that moon
that guilty phlegm
I can't cough up

and can't unsubscribe from like
the memoirs my clarion thoughts
disrupt

white ink interfering

in *The*
Guinness Book of Cloud Chamber Glyphs
and Alphabet Soup Epithets
every bliss is qualified by bliss
and every slumber's sombre

whether it's the bikini edition or
dumped in cold dark matter
I like my models clothed a bit
assuming the density of their input tends
to infinity

the same goes for the
shocking experience of shock
something
has to be left to the imagination
prior to purchase, so

with stinging hands
I turn the snow pages
to see below
shadows of ruined cathedrals
casbahs, stadia

curved tracks
footprints
something perhaps dragged
from a car
the snow volumes

have no weight
just
frontier dimensions
they're hospital patients
splayed in white

while I have no weight either
because I jettison waste.
as I fly over the plains the
refugees look up
to my merciless gaze

opera tutu

You said two words, rocks
and tree

I heard, Cézanne and zen, and thought
of a hill in France

and the argument in the patisserie
didn't matter any more

I have bread
not cake

the lines on the brow of the hill
wrinkle encouragingly

beers and bears
support me now

and in Bilbao Sumi Jo
sings to her Yankee captain

from every frame in every plane
tears flow

rembrandt's meat

in that certain land
untouched by solar gain
not mars, not earth

and not that planet love
her hot terrain
the last we'll visit

in that pure land reflected
from sequestered seas
themselves refracting skies

we screwed unthinkingly
and grunted with surprise
when it hurt or didn't

and with new positions
and permissions
explored

improbable new passages
through time and its corollaries
then afterwards

i heard a pendulum
whistling, near
you heard rain

we left the house
upon the hour
and in the woods

we found a small breeze
sly, agnostic
two-hoofed

smoking a cheroot
fingering a dryad
its rising fur

said snap me now
see where my liquor breath
rots leaves

and then we're slick and running naked
scared
and start an argument

that can't be finished
about the sacred
and profane

I grid my points
with lightning straws
through which to suck

epiphanies
you match temerity
with ambiguity, tug me

back through that
looking glass
peppered with the cracks of dreams

through which we step
like sleeping glue
possessed, to

a desert where a pyramid
of wood chips
is lit by sunset

an annunciation
I must forget
like rembrandt's meat

last a splayed
ox
first

soft skinned Saskia
cleaved to her
husband, hooked

by time
and torn in her
surrendering

once was pink

there's that word again
about time too 'cos
nothing clangs any more
it's all compressed
in that acronym format in which
the algorithm reduces
what you expect to hear and preserves
the difference
the complex timbre that reminds
some old dude of childhood
or a passage in a novel he forgot
he'd read at dusk
500 years ago in exile far inland
press PLAY and it reproduces
every nuance they recorded
of sax and chord and reedy
susurration in their state of the
art studio
and if you concentrate about
halfway through track ten you'll hear
that word again
it rhymes with silence
and if you tap it with the tip
of your middle finger regularly
it resonates with shadows
like the hum of a fast car at night
gliding between drizzling fields
where naked humans forage one of them
looks up and is dazzled by the hovering
chopper's spotlight
there's that word again
burnt into his brain drenched
with kilowatts sweetly shocking loud

curse in Klingon

wipes her brow with a plain white
handkerchief

as lightly armed
gladiactors in the rainbow arena
skate to k.d. lang

subject puts fingers in ears, sings
chap, chap, this chap, nice old chap…

I've maintained lordosis
since Christ had croup
and still my back aches but no more
navel-gazing
my body fluids circulate
my mind's alert

if most of reality's in the future
then it's time to face the music

the cognoscenti of Middle Earth
curse in Klingon
plough viridian dales

their human brothers run the gauntlet naked
past paparazzi their sparkling cameras

while memory the centrifuge
spatters ink from tabloids
in fine lines across the ceiling

rose

when you write the novel of your life

think of the cover first
imagine
being lonely in an airport bored
and there it is
the author's name in gold
the title gleaming underneath
the blurb succinct
then decide
how many pages
the more the better
maybe a thousand
you can always
trim it later
next the minor characters
with unlikely names
and scenes in places
where you've never been before
don't forget
the quality of paper
acidic
with no inserts
for photographs
someone like you
should rely on what they write
not what they do
or who happened
to say look at the camera
smile
and let's try one more time
so long
ago

live at the apollo and they shouted

after all day being dazzled dazzling
it's night for Apollo that damned lyre
of course the he and she gods

the queer gods the polyamorous of every hue
play the phantoms
of the me and you

from our blister pack of sorrows
we pop out our dei ex machinis
of the night, cry

crane me down Scotty
lower me into your black
incinerator of dreams

where the hell deep sparkles
election smoke chokes
and nothing's everywhere

darkling through the mauve that was my mind
I scry your being unkind
to what's left of the you you left behind

and now that nothing left occurs
in nothing much at all
it's time to call the sun god's favours in

improbable but likely to be true
here comes yet another dawn
for me and you

under cover of night my tar baby
portraits splash through galleries not
theirs to grace by day

why do I care more
about your active

galactic
nucleus

than what I paint now on this dark
and dizzy night?

your secret's wasted
on platonic solid me

you're stuck on a perfect day
of the perfect parts you play

so powder my maths, trickle it
onto your fresh glue life

light motive 1

liturgy of beasts and blades
whispered across your breast

nicks and scratches on what had been
the perfect surface of your thought

and feelings, stormy though they were before
that jade

and jagged knife
sliced once, and instantly revealed

what tide and time had left unsaid
the sentence of your passion

your life in deeds, at one remove
revealed

light motive 2

I read nothing in her face or maybe
a bell sounded

her hands diced for
minutes before

figurines toppled in gardens
emptied of movies and moonlight

and her thoughts
took flight across water

limb upon limb she climbed
skin upon skin was never enough

light motive 3

your fingerprints on my dreams your DNA
on my limbs
traces of you
prod
my barrier
O love
retrievable radio
I can't
get your fluid out of my throat
slick rivers close over
I breathe your imagined life

let the wound form lips and sing

at last my chance to touch the dark
mottle of your face
preceding what could be
one perfect moment of detention

you said we had to be in the zone
but we've never been in the zone
you said you felt you were disappearing
it was true

your halo negative
your last thoughts
leaking into night
so this

is my last chance to touch you
because I can't remember
what you felt like
naked

we skinny dipped three days ago
slid to the coral
stayed down too long
out of the sun

now no breath bubbles
the telepathic crackle
between our heads is faint
and awkwardly tangled in tango

where the words come from

and then in my soft porch innocuous
a sweet voice pentecostal
clear as moonlight outside Tucson

injected me with calmest night

like an angel knocked silly by plainsong
I fell among headstones fluttering I
thudded, a confused marsupial

caught in headlights
though I was driving and considered myself
invulnerable

I veered toward them
but they flew either side of me
two bikies out for a burn in the dark

or the long trek

south

of the solar system debris
zones and lava flow
and all my history

cooled into light

I'm not cured yet

last night I ripped
up by bird ways
I could not open Rilke
it was a tattered book
its pages
argued on the shelf
that untranslatable incline
dappled with shadows of gods
and equations
like walking once
down Ben Bulben in dusk
out of the tearing mist
into visible Yeats country
into the bird song static
and ripple
on over Sligo Bay

thisness

as in the ideal experiences
I rehearse shamelessly
on centre court

the podium or when the woven
fibre tautens
at the intake of your breath

thisthis
when the cello's
commentary becomes attack
violins deduplicate

& the viola cries
across
the face of its occasion

thisless I am
a blur framed by topiary
zipping
the theory of theatre
exploding
actual theatre
where thisless means
no audience

thiswith is
angel with
arquebus

taste
wine in your bread
your gag reflex gone

your white neck bent
& then
incarnadine

materiality

the vast
how hard to redact it
how hard to live
on the edge of it

hard enough
to escape
to escape the rusty
orchards

and on the edge of achieving
materiality to fail
by trying not to
not try

after... Clive James

tired of reading novels from the future
and understanding none (which
is my privilege and duty)
the maps in my eyes fade
into the earth they simulate
I choose to rename those things
provisional
precarious
transitory, which
still persist
(I assume you can
read Heidegger
on this
a wheelie bin
fanfare in the wings
the glass between us
slewed and slow the light takes years to pass)

on two tongue common

dramatic kick in the pants and away we go
a calliope on the edge of a field whistles
through leaves as spookily here
as in the sixties film Blow Up where David Hemmings
plays the photographer and Veruschka the model

but reality is as grainy as the close up of a sixties
film print they didn't have AI then to endlessly sharpen
anything they zoomed in on like leaves in slo mo trees
on the edge of a fugue you know the ones like Bach's,
Buxtehude's, whoever

by endlessly I mean without realistic limit I mean there
are still things too small to see I mean adequately visualise
like fundamental
particles not that they exist enough to be specifically
observed

like
the quanta of my thoughts before I have them
or perhaps David Foster Wallace had them
or David Hemmings or Veruschka Von Lehndorff
the point is it was a dramatic

kick in the pants like KER-BAM inside a jagged
frame in a Popeye comic I read in the
I suppose it was the fifties
tho' I forget who kicked whom
if that's correct English, anyway this kinda Germanic

fugue thing is crude because it's actually going somewhere
you listen to a fragment and you just know it's propelling stuff
in the days before propellors well
they had screws of course, didn't the Greeks
into the future... I want... thing... I mean... invent it?

Bread Street far away

In the Milton home
companion the ingrate

drowns in whisky,
his blind hands grasp the air

and sketch the gods. He gestures.
And a tent appears.

A car park. And streams
of people.

Stream to it. The guest speaker
in his chopper

looks down and is
momentarily anxious.

They're all coming to hear
him. He hovers over

his country, fields, orchards,
his onomatopoeia,

his days, his disordered
horses. Below

birds veer and
thud in aqueous humour,

giants fall between hills,
pollen drifts

on lawns.
So far.

So good. And on the stage
he'll walk on fire,

and water, which is
more difficult.

quick tarot break

for years
I yodelled
among the hills
of charmed preexistence
now it's
planked dark country

and each plank
a card
and on it many stairs
in the style of Escher offering
infinite egress
but no escape

now no more yodelling
all night I listen to the
worms
and whispers in your heart
and as I travel time
I tighten as I shrink

to a pin prick
treading on this
pin pricked planet
slipping
on your tears
the scattered dew

tourists and purists

when we were
thin
(even
past masters
slip
up)

were we fish
with no need
of hands
or the virtue
of limbs?

or angels
half full of light
spinning
unnecessary narratives
into the water?

hoisted
on blue words
didn't we know
what to say next?

calque

did you prosper on the other side of
number, deep in complex, deep in
white? deep in the run of run dog

run? did you comprehend the
other plans, the bees bebopping,
bees that chase a dog

or hive a lion recently
dismembered? you've
imagined every permutation

and now you're sure
that covenant
convenience is past

but did you dwell well
there, in infinitude, or would
you prefer another

run?

sextet

try floating in that
abstract
space

of voodoo
border
worlds

in planes of night
and ochre
phased

abrupt light
scans
your soul

an oboe plays
along a coast,
from teal courts rise

luminous
domino
desires

assuming thinking

is possible
and there are several
reasons

and a battery
here at the beginning
is elastic with

anticipation
then you can count
the days of your life

backwards from now
into the silence
of the plants

there is no other
thought bubble
worth popping

carnival of clones

just as the bright infant predicts the infinity of natural
   numbers without yet counting them so yr tomorrow
   overflows with boredom like the kingdom of rain on
   helpless heads and

while I'm in a block of marble by the shore

u hold a cube of starlight in yr hands it's leaking

u'd jammed yr fingers up those hags' dry cracks but they
   snipped yr lifeline anyway u shoulda remembered those
   fates once were nubile spinners rubbing their damp
   crotches on u but u

stayed too long

so now u lie dying I'm rereleased to touch you with

me thermodynamical zero game wand thingy it whirrs
   enough but I guess the universe'll contract as

stiff hands stir among bones to pull out pink so quick that
   slippery salmon yr heart still beating we need

to dampen these spiralling, exaggerated signs

on the origin of

first there's a purple gradient mauve from nowhere and
   from nowhere a stream of mauve tiles issues, by their
   shadows you shall know them as they turn this violet
   stem into murmurs murmuring buddy bud bud 'cos

just some spunk slipped past your thought, skipped
   schemes its rich head wrigglers semi cell packs jacked in
   milky skeins their blind gradients one of them merges
   with a giant globe rises through the transept of all
   possible praise 'cos

every accident is frozen every event locked forever in the
   database of all that was so why do I spend so much time-
   and-energy trying to reinvent it the...

drum roll...

past? 'cos

yeah, it's not an unrealistic captain's call late in the closing
   quarter merely trying to invent my little version of 'how
   this game goes' in the present never mind 'what comes
   next' for now is now is

Easter Saturday and all of Melbourne's stop start traffic to
   the shack shops sport footie roos dogs get to family
   mum dad lover lonely epidemic kids it's Holy Saturday
   holy smoke windscreens dissolve in light for what
   comes next? the furnace resurrection redux

a moment too soon for us as in all moments and no time
   returns 'cos

on the origin of old stone crosses of the Vale of Clwyd

the last stanza by Rev Elias Owen MA 1886

stop work down tools void bells book
a seat
at Radio City Music Hall
for an evening with Dead Can Dance

or a standup in a club that joker at the end of the bed
    prattling like the clappers, fading, fading
ghosts in alumni annals
play Sibelius's second where the horns burr or Brahms' first
    quoting the Cambridge chimes, d'ya like horns?
the script's not tight, the characters blurt lines that don't
    ring true, the actors embarrassed, like

when God made and Nature put
the scent of glue in that dark room
cardboard cutouts perspex towers, gates with pinholes
    focussing interior scenes on many walls, pearls in pools,
    mouths singing
no – pets – allowed

stop work down tools the moon rises over Gotham City
innocents abroad gasp
as the moonlight papers up the cracks between the
    skyscrapers and the tenements
and all is white and white and white and white

and on Shrove Tuesday
boys went about with two stones as clappers and when
    opposite a farm house
clapped away with all their might and received for their
    pains a gift
of eggs

Antares 2

look there it is up there
and then the beguile
few minds in words contend

the belt of being
the wallpaper
round the warm dry box they sleep in

now there's a confession
from each disordered kitchen take
all words antiquated and anti thought like

once were dead
and make them live again
or is it just too soon to tell

tonight

the mute tv
in the peri
phery the little
phones bark

the fridge
hums my ear
s ring there
are many lights

i eat yog
hurt and hurt
enough i am to
drink more wine

to night i
move in vast
steps i am
the only one

in the house
therefore thou art
not
here and

there is no
space you can
inhabit
here

i drink more wine
and photographs
inside your

dark interior flicker
loud enough
and long

medical insight

i thought even the surgeon has intestines but i couldn't help
    looking when she bent forward i saw through the gap
    at the side of her scrubs her fluoro pink knickers

but her blue balloons of stinging green liquid got stuck in
    my mind and her squeezaholic dumpity dumper her
    heart corpuscles zooming with oxygen through
    chambers and on to her brain

this kept me occupied till i forgot the dead loved one on the
    trolley but that flash of pink was like one spelling
    mistake in a giant and otherwise perfect book

it resonated into the real the faint whiff of life i almost forgot
    in the months of disease and despair i knew what'd come
    next it was ok I could handle the grief loss pain

that i still can't feel though i try

it's ten years now and in the mall the opera the office and
    even at sea i'm surrounded by organs of efficient desire
    that aren't me

into the flower mountains

now the sharp air the welding light the novel in a million steps

imagining the wind imagining clouds

imagining mountains of flowers imagining a highway
imagining vehicles ploughing through flowers

below the snow line currawongs concatenate high trees
brown top stringybarks blue gums peppermints

all glazed by an imaginary pianist articulating minute
photographs on pianos in a factory full of themes and
variations of the heroes of the hour

I can't believe I'm not that piano in my richter room non
trompe l'oeil all for the price of opening my eyes but

I'm walking on flower mountains

another late de Kooning

the fact that I didn't want any of it
except for an endless John Adams riff
folded into a thousand paper planes one
for each day of grief and you

didn't want any of it either being
post mortem and beyond
need or memory the fact that
the family only wanted bits

and all our bright plain days were
out of sight and undermined
while in my hand I gripped
a wand

ready to ignite all
that moved or should have shone
the fact that now the truth would
never tell itself because

no story needs itself to sing
…
or I'm post mortem too
which casts a different light on things

well look who's here

pissed again I failed to see
death and her maggots
pull into the driveway
pissed – as in…

being slowly converted into a painting
by David Hockney
of lapdogs or a canyon
better than being plastered…

up a long last judgement
to balefully eyeball forever
tourists and cardinals
in a tomb that's open all hours…

so death sat in her can
and lisped into the radio
recurrent affairs preprogrammed since
the dawn of remember when…

maggots consumed her soft
interior she smiled
that ambiguous hi that famous come on
come on over…

through the tough glass the opening in the wall
into the next valley
where the silence
blows

onward ocean

each day your clothes
torn from a book

about wild bright over
onward ocean

as if Linnaean
as if everything were speechless

species or
accidents

that couldn't happen
this time

Phocion's ashes

who could stem
violin
increments before
entimement?

in the abyss of culture
the abyss of flowers
my hand
flashes through synecdoche

a window opens
its gravity warps
my sabre
thrums

if this portal's my
portrait in infinity
it's a simulation
in an infinite regress

and I'm thinking now it's
in another simulated now
my widow gathers me
in her hot delighted hands

after the crash (Coalbrookdale)

rogue fader
I shade into floral tributes
diluting the perfume of dying
Abraham Darbys

yeah, I'd been raised by humans, too
too late now to do anything but
imitate their elocuted
grunts – like you, I guess

I'd prefer transcription
into their smaller worlds
their empty animal acts
like titles of movies

never made, biopsies that never
got to the lab
that could have been, and almost were
my carved out lives

shot, exterior

by their scars you shall know them
the versions of you
the parade of automata
tooling over the landscape
on various legs
you cast bitter

aspersions, not worthy
not worthy at all, it's not
how you were brought up
to look down on
the remnants
of me

there's wind in the trees
a change coming the
edge of a front
the edge of the massive
sum of your lives
I am afraid

to stay here the beauty
not yours to share
any more than
my rights
being reduced to refusal
and I don't know the consequence

of staying though I
thrash through the odds
in my oddball way
ignoring
your vast therapeutic your love my last
chance in the sun

open top bus tour of Tourette, it's

better to tour
at night
by firelight

than in the sun
with your sunglasses
shading the shapes

while shadows escape
24/7
you're

periodically
torn into small
pieces

to drift
over
couples

or the little
saint in the pool
the sea anemone

over her waving
head
the incoming

particles
whatever
make sense

for a saint's day
a little expense
worth wonders

mementos
buying causes
for peace

meanwhile my galaxies
quickly
depopulate

I'm gifted
with an indolence
of privilege

and escape
death
daily though

my tongue was
nailed to a tree
on fire

then, torn during
the daring
escape,

its forked
speech
flailed and

the machines
and my people
were one

biomorph 1

benighted queen
less desired than dreamed of
how come your daliesquerie
drifts my radar?

you might writhe
like a heart in a throat
but possessing neither
could ease your propulsion

I know you're all ear
and have waited long
for this thought
I insert in you now

please accept it
in the spirit
in which
it's pretended

I, Ro

get a life, you tell me
but I want to parse my life
disambiguate it
not like you
(my costar!)
you
run on a parallel track
you don't poke along
whistling show tunes
whirring through your conundrums
you tackle the day
like it's your last chance to forget
whereas I have no memories
to speak of
no morning symphonies
or cries from the savannah
my track record's up front, out there
for all to see
including you
who invented me

not Green Lantern

I'm the morph
you heard about
on late night tv
I turn myself into
(for example) the
Incredible Hulk or Gina Lollobrigida
(google these if you're not sure
who I mean)

the transitions take months
and are quite comical
(when my dick disappears, for instance,
but is not yet its
counterpart)

I've got a following among small boys
and older women
with an independent income
you can find me on Digimon cards and giant
billboards (I was once revealed as Michael Jordan
50 storeys high
I *was* Michael Jordan)
or on the faces of expensive ladies watches
changing
slower than weather

but my little trick
is inherently dissatisfying
I want to go beyond
the silky poetics
of the human genome
like

a dung beetle in New South Wales or a
candelabra in Zurich
something challenging
(the transitions now grotesque,

going beyond the animate
is my chief desire)

once wandered

walking backwards to Persepolis
I track your thighs' diaspora

I sniff their chords, their contumely
piques the desert air

their least unseemly strides
just can't be true

I sum their feathered instants
the curve flies vertical

lifted far beyond the evidence
the past stares down

its folds on folds
fold

heaven's narrative
but nothing like you think

the cyborg ballet rapper wraps
shadows over every kid who thinks that

gravity
won't hurt them

non-realists they pad
rainforest paths to ruins

wandering thighs
black music

good reasons
once, for living

pure durum

lately I seem to be
always driving from
or to funerals
teenagers farting in the back
oldies in the front
hanging out
for a cup of tea
and profiteroles

I want to switch on the radio but
instead we reminisce
about the recently
deceased
in our heads we
reverse
the video
of their lives
all that spaghetti
uncurling
stiffening in the pot
slipping
back into cellophane packets
sealed
placed in the cupboard
the supermarket bag
the warehouse truck
factory silo field
pure durum wheat
soil rain air
sunlight
drenching down on an
Australian plain

don't get me wrong
I don't resile
from the complexity of life
I'm sure everything's
multifactorial
hypertextual

and full of broken links

but it's nice to think
as in their end
so their beginning

why can't I

be like that?

more about the art of

at the mercy of this stream
glimpsed between leaves
profligate with oxygen
babbling
in galleries in the mill race
beneath my sternum
you spin, mildly
electric

at the behest of whispers
you play piano
far underground
sign off de facto
fault lines
bathe
mummy swathes
in fluorescing bacteria

but I just want to eat bread
sip moonshine
sup on the faint
movement of your
décolletage while you
breathe, Delilah
and I finger my
shears

m-m-m-mahler

it's too late to listen to Mahler
after a lifetime of movies
surprise is cliché
and thrills don't

and too late to read
unlimited novels
with similar
excuses

even Elisabeth Schwarzkopf's
honey
won't
heal me

what's left
is the aching
art of what's left
of the 21st century

as we slide through
apocalypse
into
silence

bang again bang

in the heavy metal kingdom
of the dog and the bee
heaven's a trillion

hours away but for you
and me baby whole
minutes might elapse

before we click that
offer dangling there that
fruit on the tree whatever

offends singularity
don't be fooled by curves
the way they approach

and recede their feminine
forms implicit across time
only once were we vertical

and once was enough

bob, dart

play your clavier close
to my ear
spit in the funnel
squeeze it night

spray grace
and oracular
force
churn milk then

fan your yawns
into a child
who wipes her mouth
with the back of her hand

the light from the nearest star
burns her brow
as she blinks in
your accessible smoke

among all

the old white cis folx I know
I'll soon be the one
who's oldest, whitest, cis-est, so

don't call me a cunt
or silly
or a prick and

stupid
it's just my turn
on the pyre

of necessity
heat seeking
alternate titles

for the ceaseless moments
we're caught in the gravity strands
of when we're bereft

it's
easy
for stars to be aligned

at least for any two
the shortest distance between us
shall we call it straight

our lips our legs our
polysyllables not
withstanding

the volcanoes of lava
the boulders of pumice
bobbing on oceans of grief?

thinking again about

your face
how it reminds me of
my face

though you're
alive
you carry your dead

heaped
on your shoulders
while I carry mine

on my back
and if your load's
too heavy, I tell you

remember
it's OK to breathe
it's permissible

to sing while you're sailing
you say who am I
to give such unwarranted advice

and I tell you
I know nothing about sailing
not

even which way the wind blows
my face being
numb to such things

as breezes
I could peel
the invisible mud from my face

but that would defeat the purpose
of always trying to sail
into the wind

stupidly not realising
it so frequently
changes

that morning

when you ran through our open door and it was glass
your face opened
Silver ran barefoot across shards, wrapped her shirt round
    your head
to hold your cheek in place
I touched triple zero
your mother hadn't moved
she'd seen
her firstborn sliced into daylight
it took only a moment
for you to bloom

your uber has arrived

a bugle in the forest
the midsummer bungle blasts
cis folx to faeries, giants,
donkeys, ocelots, constellations of

archaea

at last there is no logic
at least the math is plane
a blockchain sublimes
a cloud of digits
steams

and small children stream on holiday
to distant centuries
memories
maybe

felicities

been there thought that

it doesn't matter that I wrote no poems
down all those damned deciduous years
Gwen Harwood wrote every thought I had
burnt them in song
and made me glad

now she's been dead these many years I'm
catching thoughts again
they jangle in my brain
jagged icons
of accumulated pain

it's my turn now
to spit my weak water into the wind
to growl at crows
and wade against
the undertows

and Gwen returns
each year to shine on Bruny
a comet preceded by her tale of dusty light
this is her flesh in which
she has seen God

reply to the ghost

so there are lights in common places
eastward violas sheen ephemera
bars, beams of clouds intimate

illimitable particularity
each leaf in subtle momenta
russetting

a slip of a star ship
flits my mind
girls daisy chain galaxies

boys
discombobulated
scratch dust between

disturbing destinies
and late in a day of
din

you dive
and swim the air
a few metres

flailing
then hit
the earth

lissom somnambulist
now defy with your art
we who cannot witness it

your unlimited genres
play out
unhesitating

you tightrope
walk
through dark

while we tread
a narrow curve
from edifice to edifice

with no way back
your argosies
depend dim winds

short sonnet

but the bears bit Goldilocks
mauled her with their mitts
savaged her without passion
objectively

I kissed her goodbye in the viewing room
then rolled her head from side to side
to see how loose it was
surprising, the zero resistance of death

the button from her nightdress
was pressed into the asphalt by her fall
rain and traffic did not remove it
only my fingers

this butter, I did not want to swallow it
none of us did

the memento tinge

on things that should otherwise
be burnt

or buried
or recycled

into benign
compounds

leaving
nothing but a memory

of smoke
like lovers who smoked

but were otherwise
satisfactory

I'm sorry
I should be specific

and name the articles
their vivid

catalogue of virtues
and bitterness

but I got rid of the lot
and the incompetent chords

of my memory
cannot bring them back

so I'll just have to say
I made it all up

this life I once had that
they're 'celebrating' now

while my gardens of junk
remain

it's the idea of the girl

the girl
the idea of the girl in the west
of the west
the idea
of a girl sleeping
it's the idea of her sleeping
she sleeps an idea
in a white dress in a bed
a bed
she sleeps in the west in a bed
she's an idea
sung by Salli Terri
on a record
sung on a record on a record player
in 1969 in a bedroom a room
in 1969 the windows
the windows of the room face
the windows face north
to other windows
facing north
I lie white
in a white dress in a bed in an idea in the west
in a song a
traditional song
an autobiographical love song
I blink at the ceiling
lit by a lamp
running across it meandering like
a tributary of the Avon
a line
the warm milk of
my lover seeps over my legs
my brown legs in a dress
it's a night dress a
wedding dress in the west

it trickles
and the fine line
the fine line on the ceiling's
like the groove in the record it's Salli
Terri the salty singer she will sing
this song forever
in the groove in the line he
turns from the window
he turns he
wants me
always wants me
he always he's
always north
looking through the window
another window
to the north, in the north
two men
are landing on the moon
their voices
crackling still in our heads they
descend to the sea
to the sea I can't
I can't remember the sea
of equilibrium
they descend they're close
still flying north too fast they nearly
crash
on the moon the moon the
cold ovum calm
poised
planetesimal
the men land they admire they
bounce towards the curved horizon
I'm in a dress in a bed
I'm an idea of a girl
in a bed
in the west country
my love is a love

of high degree
he'll leave me he'll leave
wading through
memory
he wants me again and again
I'm simply his
idea of a girl in a bed
in a room staring
at the ceiling the fine
line in the
ceiling
the dawn coming
the lover coming standing
the window waiting
waiting for the dawn on the moon
the men bouncing we saw it on tv
anything is possible
now

Regard du Fils sur le Fils

the bird in the mirror the child
dreams the mirror the bird the rays
the Valium ghost between silver empty the
shards of bird brides mirror the child
steps in a spacewalk stealing the stars
the bars of light and silence when
only the child's eyes see the child

Par Lui tout a été fait

walk on the bridge in the wind
in the dark 20 metres down gulls
beat upstream then wheel away 50 metres
down the water's black candy the event
horizon so it's back to that old
recipe for disaster graveyard of mothers the
years being stromatolites in seas of despair

Regard de la Croix

in the library the rainforest I sang
but not a human voice came out
a god not my god I've heard
her voice before turning the pages ululating
among the gums his voice was different
it split the wood in Mandelbrot patterns
spat the cream my brain again again

Regard des Hauteurs

the girl with willow pattern eyes ran
on a seamless beach it was 1964
two sandpipers kept a safe distance before
her on bright vibrating legs meandering then
broke into flight slipped over the slick
the wash the breakers as the girl
fell she saw them in vertical climb

Regard de l'esprit de Joie

two stroke aria chainsaw in the hills
then the shuffling silence after the credits
then Marilyn Monroe in her sewn-on happy
birthday Mr President dress wriggles onto the
stage (gasps, pauses) faces the audience opens
her mouth a tremendous voice comes out
O Freunde…

Regard des Anges

genetically modified genitalia glow in the dark
virtual sensations expand the wave front beats
into the waiting host legions of fans
scream for rock idols they shoot intimate
social text graphics porn they flash swarming
multidimensional strings of massively redundant digitally
recombinant
information into darkness the camera obscura shunt

Regard des Prophètes, des Bergers et des Mages

luminous gifts but it's hard to remember
who gave what the manger's empty the
cartoon comet's gone the camels doped the
prophets dumb and the shepherds settling among
their sheep again count their blessings while
they can – these mushrooms which have spored
strictly for one night only by demand

Je dors, mais mon coeur veille

to the besieged governor of the clouds
in the year of the cuckoo (after
I walked in moonlight and pricked by
the wind a particle entered my bloodstream
and proceeded by flashlight through crimson video
malls into the limbic) your call is
important but all our operators are busy

Regard de l'Église d'Amour

the view from the flight deck's all roses
wave upon wave of full blown Albertines
emerge from the fingerprints the vacuum galaxies
in soft convoy pink under starshine they
parade their slow lips parted they sing
of the wind in the trees and
the scent of earth then and forever

notes to the next

I am moving
where there should be
a blade of grass
or an animal

a human with an animal
could be a new nation
beneath
a weight

there is an enormous
swallowing
I am moving
before a lie materialises

could I find a minimal animal
a code
exploited exploiting
to be my paradigm in thin days?

better than bridges

it's better than bridges
to swim across ignorant summer
in this this only life

transubstantiation 3

when humankind
and all her spawn
galactic empires
and so on
are gone

and Shakespeare never breathed

and no star stirs
without a bug remarks
a new event
in its dominion

and children never swam

and Eve and Adam
have not yet sinned
nor ever will

and lovers never died

nor loved nor sighed

and the smoke from the cherry wood burning on the shore
never drifted over the bay
the day I rowed
to Maria

then new scents will fill the heavens
and with whatever tentacles of fire
new intelligences
caress their skies

they will